WATERY WORLDS

SEASHORE LIFE

by Jinny Johnson

A⁺

Smart Apple Media

Published by Smart Apple Media
P.O. Box 3263
Mankato, MN 56002

Printed in the United States of America at Corporate Graphics, in North Mankato, Minnesota.

Library of Congress Cataloging-in-Publication Data
Johnson, Jinny, 1949-
  Seashore life / Jinny Johnson.
    p. cm. -- (Watery worlds)
  Includes index.
  ISBN 978-1-59920-501-4 (library binding)
  1. Seashore animals--Juvenile literature. I. Title.
  QL122.2.J63 2012
  591.769'9--dc22
                        2010039111

Created by Appleseed Editions, Ltd.
Designed by Hel James
Illustrations by Graham Rosewarne
Edited by Mary-Jane Wilkins
Picture research by Su Alexander

Picture credits
Contents page Tuulijumala/Shutterstock; 4 Roseanne Smith/Shutterstock; 5 Emjay Smith/Shutterstock;
6 Sean Bolton/Alamy, 6/7 background Stephen Meese/Shutterstock, 7 Timothy Epp/Shutterstock; 8
Bradley Allen Murrell/Shutterstock, 8/9 background Stephen Aaron Rees/Shutterstock, 9t Ekaterina
Pokrovsky/Shutterstock, b R Gino Santa Maria/Shutterstock; 10 Cary Kalscheuer/Shutterstock, 10/11
background Stephen Meese, 11 Tatiana Belova/Shutterstock; 12 Rico/Shutterstock; 13t JonMilnes/
Shutterstock, b Joe Belanger/Shutterstock; 14 Cigdem Cooper/Shutterstock, 14/15 background
Tuulijumala/Shutterstock, 15t Vittorio Bruno/Shutterstock, b Abraham Badenhorst; 16 A & S Aakjaer/
Shutterstock, 16/17 background Stephen Aaron Rees/Shutterstock, 17t Ian Scott/Shutterstock, b David
Dohnal/Shutterstock; 18 Neelsky/Shutterstock, 18/19 background Stephen Meese/Shutterstock, 19t
EcoPrint/Shutterstock, bl Sergey Khachatryan/Shutterstock, br Nikita Tiunov/Shutterstock; 20 Andrea
Leone/Shutterstock, 20/21 background Tuulijumala/Shutterstock, 21t Kirsten Wahlquist/Shutterstock, b
Andrea Haase/Shutterstock; 22 Nina B /Shutterstock, 22/23 background Michael Zysman/Shutterstock,
23 Rebvt/Shutterstock; 24 Vatikaki/Shutterstock; 25t Heiko Kiera/Shutterstock, b Rich Carey/
Shutterstock; 26 Hugh Landsdown/Shutterstock, 26/27 background Frontpage/Shutterstock, 27t Marco
Alegria/Shutterstock, b Bernhard Richter; 29 Holger W/Shutterstock; 30/31 background Tuulijumala/
Shutterstock
Front Cover: main image Stephen Aaron Rees/Shutterstock, below left to right: Ecoprint/Shutterstock, A
& S Aakjaer/Shutterstock, JonMilnes/Shutterstock

DAD0050
3-2011

9 8 7 6 5 4 3 2 1

Contents

Life Between the Tides

The seashore is where land and ocean water meet. Twice a day, the tide goes in and out. The waves surge up sandy beaches or crash onto rocky shores.

The seashore might seem to be a difficult place for animals to live. Sometimes, they are exposed to the wind and sun. At other times, they are underwater.

At high tide, waves travel up the beach and crash against rocks and cliffs.

In fact, the seashore is bursting with life in the shallow water close to the land and on the shore itself. Some seashore creatures survive because they have hard shells to protect them; others live in burrows or take shelter among the seaweed.

Amazing!

Almost all (about 90 percent) of sea creatures live in coastal areas.

At low tide, much of the beach is open to the sun and wind. Some creatures hide in pools. Others close their shells to protect themselves.

Guess What?
The moon controls the tides on Earth. It pulls the water in the oceans toward it by a force called gravity.

Rock Clingers

Not all sea creatures swim and dive. Some spend nearly all their time in one place, often on rocks on the seashore. Many have special ways of clinging to their homes so they don't get washed away as the tide goes in and out.

Limpets, barnacles, and mussels start life as tiny creatures that float in the sea as they grow. When they are fully grown, they settle on a rock or other surface. Barnacles and mussels do not move again. Limpets do move around to feed on **algae**, a kind of seaweed, but only when the rocks are wet or covered by the tide.

A limpet clings to surfaces with a part of its body called its foot, which acts like a sucker to keep it in place. Some limpets make their home on boats or even whales!

Limpets leave a sticky trail when they move around so they can always find their way back to the same spot.

Amazing!

Guess What?

Do you know how a barnacle feeds? When it is covered by water at high tide, a barnacle opens its shell at the top and sticks out its feathery arms. It uses these to gather tiny bits of food from the water.

Sticky threads hold a mussel onto its rocky home and help it stay put through the roughest tides.

Hidden in the Sand

The sand on the shore is made by the waves pounding on bits of rock and shell over many years. A sandy beach may look very empty with few places for creatures to live. In fact, there are many animals, but most of them live below the surface.

Lots of lugworms live on sandy beaches. They live in burrows shaped like tubes. Look for little dips in the sand—a sure sign of a lugworm burrow. Different kinds of clams make burrows, too.

A razor clam can dig fast. It can bury itself in less than seven seconds when it is in danger.

Amazing!

Look for lugworm burrows like these. Each burrow has a little pile of waste next to it.

Crabs sometimes scuttle across the beach and then burrow under the sand. Little beach hoppers or beach fleas hide in the sand during the day. They come out at night to feed on anything washed up by the tide.

Crabs have 10 legs. They swim well and can walk on the seabed.

WATCH OUT!

We all love sandy beaches, but we can damage them easily. Lots of people walking around can disturb burrows and flatten the sand so it becomes hard and compact. Cars and dune buggies do more serious harm. Litter on the beach may hurt creatures that try to eat it, so always take your garbage home.

Life in a Tide Pool

When the tide goes out, some creatures stay behind in little pools left in dips and hollows in the rocks. The pool has to be quite deep so it doesn't dry up on a hot day. There are plenty of hiding places for snails, crabs, and prawns.

Look for sea anemones in tide pools. They look more like flowers than animals, but they are **predators** and catch other animals to eat. A sea anemone catches its **prey** with its stinging **tentacles** and pulls it into its mouth. It spends most of its life fixed to one place by a sucking disk at the end of its body.

Starfish, sea urchins, and sea anemones are some of the creatures living in this tide pool.

Guess What?

Clownfish can live around a sea anemone without being harmed by the anemone's stinging tentacles. This is good for both animals. The fish is safe from other predators as it cleans scraps and algae off the anemone. In return, the anemone cannot harm the fish.

Most sea anemones are less than 2 inches (3 cm) long, but some grow to 59 inches (1.5 m).

Amazing!

A sea anemone's tentacles pull prey into its mouth at the center of its body. The anemone also draws in its tentacles when it is out of the water at low tide.

Seashore Fish

Lots of fish live in the shallow waters just off the seashore. Among them are wrasse, seahorses, blennies, and gobies. Any of these might swim by your feet as you splash in the sea.

Gobies and blennies also live in tide pools. The fins on a goby's belly are joined together to make a kind of sucking disk. This helps the fish cling to a rock so it is not swept away by crashing waves.

This goby is clinging to a rock with the help of the special fins on its belly.

Guess What?

The male seahorse is a very caring dad. The female seahorse lays her eggs into a pouch on the male's body. He keeps the eggs safe until they hatch. The tiny seahorses then swim out of his pouch.

Amazing!

Some wrasse are also known as cleaner fish. They take away dead skin, scales, and little creatures called **parasites** from larger fish. Some even swim into the mouth of larger fish to clean their teeth.

13

Slugs, Snails, and Octopuses

Snails, sea slugs, and octopuses look different from each other, but they all belong to the same group of creatures called **mollusks**. Periwinkles are sea snails; you can see them on rocks and in tide pools on every beach.

Sea slugs are snails without a shell and are more brightly colored than land slugs. Sea slugs live in all parts of the ocean, but a lot of them live in coastal waters. They hunt other creatures, such as anemones, **sponges**, and even other sea slugs.

Some sea slugs change color depending on what they eat. If a sea slug eats a red sponge, it turns red.

Amazing!

An octopus is much larger than a sea slug. It has a pouch-like body and eight arms, which are lined with suckers. Octopuses often hide under rocks in shallow water close to the shore, watching for prey such as crabs and clams.

Guess What?

An octopus likes to stay hidden from its enemies as well as from the prey it sneaks up on. It can change the color and pattern of its skin almost instantly to match its surroundings, making it very hard to see.

Coastal Birds

Gannets, pelicans, and other coastal birds do not live in the sea. They spend their lives on the shore and find their food in the water. They eat mainly fish and squid and have their own ways of catching food.

The gannet flies high over the water, looking out for any sign of fish. If it sees one, the gannet dives down into the sea with its wings held back neatly to **streamline** its body.

A gannet snatches fish from the sea with its dagger-like beak.

Amazing!

A gannet can dive into the water at up to 62 miles (100 km) per hour.

A cormorant dives from the water surface to catch fish.

WATCH OUT!

Oil spills and other **pollution** can harm shore birds. Oil damages the birds' feathers, and other chemicals make them ill. The birds may also swallow cigarette butts, plastic bags, and other litter, which can kill them.

Cormorants chase their prey very fast underwater and return to the surface to eat their catch. Oystercatchers look for food on the shoreline. They pick up shellfish such as oysters and clams with their long beaks.

An oystercatcher picks up a mussel to eat the soft flesh inside the shell.

17

Crabs, Shrimp, and Lobsters

These creatures are part of a group of animals called **crustaceans**. Most live in the sea. A crustacean has a shell that protects its soft body. It also has two sets of feelers, or **antennae**, and three pairs of mouthparts, as well as many legs.

Lobsters and crabs are large crustaceans with strong shells and big pincers. They use the pincers to break open the shells of their prey. With five pairs of legs, they can scuttle over rocks and the seabed as well as swim. Shrimp have much lighter shells and long antennae that help them find tiny bits of food in the water.

A lobster can live as long as 50 years and keeps growing all through its life.

Amazing!

The ghost crab's eyes are on short stalks to help it spot prey.

Guess What?

A hermit crab doesn't have a hard shell like other crabs. It lives in a shell left by another creature, such as a periwinkle or other snail. As it grows bigger, it leaves its shell for a larger one.

The striped cleaner shrimp eats tiny creatures and dead skin off other animals.

Seals and Sea Lions

These animals live in the sea, but they are not fish. They are **mammals**, like cats, dogs, and monkeys. Although they live in the sea, they cannot breathe in water and have to come to the surface to take a breath of air.

Seals and sea lions have flippers that help them swim. Their bodies are covered with fur and a thick layer of fat called **blubber**, which keeps them warm in the coldest sea. These animals spend most of their time in the water. Sometimes they come on land to lie on rocks in the sun or to **mate** and give birth to their young.

Amazing!

If a sea lion is feeling chilly on a sunny day, it sticks a flipper out of the water to soak up some heat from the sun.

Guess What?

The sea otter, another sea-living mammal, has learned how to use a tool to open shellfish. When a sea otter finds a clam, it also picks up a rock. It then floats on its back and bangs the clam with the rock until the shell breaks open.

Female Australian sea lions give birth to just one pup at a time. The mother feeds and cares for her pup for up to a year.

Marine Iguanas

These giant iguanas are the only lizards that live in the sea. Their home is the rocky shores of the Galapagos Islands off the coast of South America. They grow up to 5 feet (1.5 m) long.

The marine iguana looks fierce, but it feeds on algae, a type of seaweed. It scrapes its food off rocks with its small, sharp teeth. It swims and dives well and can stay under water for up to an hour. When it comes out of the cold water, it **basks** on the rocks on the shore to warm itself up.

Amazing!

A marine iguana swallows lots of salt water, but it has special **glands** that help it get rid of salt from its body. When the iguana sneezes, a spray of salt comes out.

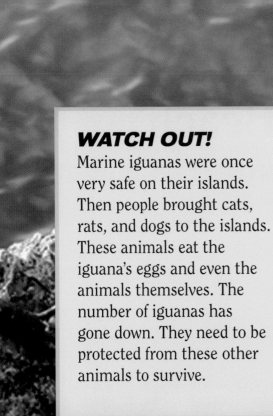

WATCH OUT!

Marine iguanas were once very safe on their islands. Then people brought cats, rats, and dogs to the islands. These animals eat the iguana's eggs and even the animals themselves. The number of iguanas has gone down. They need to be protected from these other animals to survive.

Salt from the iguana's sneezes lands on its head and looks like a little white hat.

Nesting on the Beach

Some of the biggest of all turtles live in the sea. A turtle has a shell to protect its body, like a land tortoise, but it has long flippers instead of legs. There are seven different kinds of sea turtles.

Turtles find their food in the water and spend nearly all their lives in the sea. Females come to land to lay their eggs. They swim to nesting beaches, often making a very long journey. The turtle then drags herself up onto land, digs a pit, and lays her eggs.

A turtle covers her clutch of eggs with sand to hide them from hungry predators.

Birds eat many baby turtles before they make it to the sea.

WATCH OUT!

All sea turtles are now rare, and some are in danger of disappearing forever. Many are killed by accident in fishing nets, and people also catch turtles to eat or for their shells. Turtles are also harmed by pollution. Many choke on plastic bags, which they try to eat, thinking they are jellyfish.

She goes back to the sea, leaving her eggs to stay warm in the pit. When the young hatch from the eggs, they have to make their way out of the nest and down to the sea.

A green turtle beats its flippers like wings as it swims.

Amazing!

The biggest sea turtle is the leatherback. It weighs more than three grown-up people and eats mainly jellyfish.

Life in a Mangrove Swamp

Mangrove swamps are a very special kind of seashore world on some tropical coasts. Mangrove trees can live with their roots in salt water, unlike other trees.

Fiddler crabs and many kinds of fish, such as mudskippers and archerfish, shelter among the roots of mangrove trees. Some feed on the leaves and bits of bark that fall from the trees. Egrets, anhingas, and other fish-eating birds visit the mangroves to find food. The largest of all mangrove creatures are the saltwater crocodiles, which live in swamps in southeast Asia and northern Australia.

Guess What?

The mudskipper fish can move around out of water for a short time. At low tide, it hops along over the mud with the help of its fins. Some mudskippers can even climb trees.

The male fiddler crab has an extra-large claw. He waves the large claw to let females know he is ready to mate.

Amazing!

Saltwater crocodiles are the largest crocodiles in the world—and the most dangerous. The biggest measure up to 23 feet (7 m)—longer than three people lying head to toe.

World Oceans: Atlantic

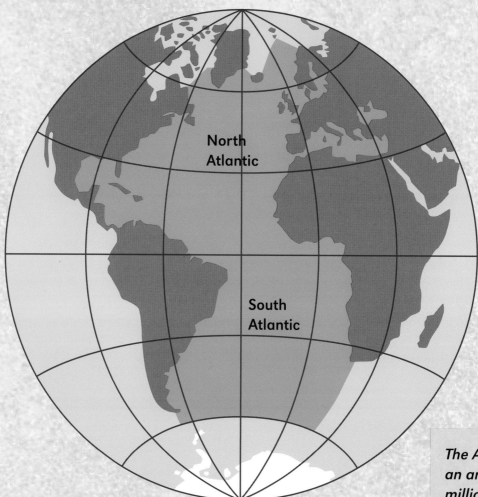

North
Atlantic

South
Atlantic

The Atlantic is the second largest ocean in the world. It covers one-fifth of Earth's surface. The ocean lies between North and South America to the west and Europe and Africa in the east. It includes the Caribbean Sea, the Mediterranean Sea, the North Sea, and the Black Sea. It reaches to the Arctic Ocean in the north and the Southern Ocean in the south.

The Atlantic covers an area of 29,630 million square miles (76,762 million sq km). It's six times larger than the United States.

Atlantic Facts

The shortest Atlantic crossing is between Senegal in Africa and northeastern Brazil in South America.

The average depth of the Atlantic is 12,010 feet (3,660 m). If the seven tallest buildings in the world were stacked on top of each other in the ocean, the top one would just peek above the surface.

The deepest point of the Atlantic is the Puerto Rico Trench, which is an amazing 27,985 feet (8,530 m) deep. Even Mount Everest, the world's highest mountain, would almost disappear in the trench.

Many of the world's largest rivers flow into the Atlantic, including the Mississippi, the Congo, and the Amazon.

This is a modern replica of the Santa Maria. *It was the largest of the three ships on Christopher Columbus's first voyage across the Atlantic in 1492.*

Glossary

algae
a type of simple green plant that lives in water

antennae
a pair of long, thin body parts on the head of
an animal such as a shrimp; antennae help it
to sense things around it.

bask
to lie in the sun or other warmth

blubber
a layer of fat covering the body of a marine
mammal such as a seal or a whale; the fat
helps to keep the animal warm.

crustacean
one of a group of animals that includes crabs,
lobsters, and shrimp; most have a tough outer shell.

gland
a part of an animal's body that makes substances
or does particular things

mammal
a warm-blooded animal that feeds its babies with
milk from its own body and has hair or fur

mate
when male and female animals pair up, or
mate, to produce young

mollusk
one of a group of animals that includes clams, mussels, and octopuses; most have a hard shell.

parasites
small creatures that live on or in the bodies of larger animals

pollution
the introduction of things that damage the natural world, such as litter and oil

predator
an animal that hunts and kills other animals to eat

prey
an animal hunted and eaten by another animal

sponge
a very simple animal that lives in water

streamline
to make a shape that moves easily through air or water

tentacles
a long body part, usually around the mouth, used for holding prey or food

Index